MILWAUKEE
BREWERS

STARS, STATS, HISTORY, AND MORE!

BY K. C. KELLEY

The Child's World®
childsworld.com

Published by The Child's World®
1980 Lookout Drive • Mankato, MN 56003-1705
800-599-READ • www.childsworld.com

ISBN 9781503828292
LCCN 2018944843

Printed in the United States of America
PA02392

Photo Credits:
Cover: Joe Robbins (2).
Inside: AP Images: 9, 17, David Durochik 29;
Newscom: Quinn Harris/Icon Sportswire 6, John Sleezer/
TNS 10, Bill Greenblatt/UPI 19, Brian Kersey/UPI 20,
Nick Wosika/Icon SW 24, Tony Quinn/Icon SW 27; Joe
Robbins 5, 13, 14, 23.

About the Author

K.C. Kelley is a huge sports
fan who has written more
than 100 books for kids. His
favorite sport is baseball.
He has also written about
football, basketball, soccer,
and even auto racing! He lives
in Santa Barbara, California.

On the Cover

Main photo: Outfielder Ryan Braun
Inset: Hall of Fame legend
Hank Aaron

CONTENTS

GO, BREWERS!

Milwaukee Brewers fans are patient! They have been cheering for their team since 1970. The team has gone all that time without a **World Series** win! Today's Brewers want to change that. The team has a bunch of great young players. They have improved four seasons in a row. Is the World Series trophy coming to Milwaukee? Let's meet the battling Brewers!

Ryan Braun has been a star for the Brewers since 2007. ➤

WHO ARE THE BREWERS?

The Brewers play in the National League (NL). That group is part of Major League Baseball (MLB). MLB also includes the American League (AL). There are 30 teams in MLB. The winner of the NL plays the winner of the AL in the World Series. The Brewers have only been in one World Series. Their fans are hoping for more soon.

◄ *Jhoulys Chacin from Venezuela is one of the top Brewers pitchers.*

WHERE THEY CAME FROM

In 1969, a new team joined MLB. The Seattle Pilots lasted only one season! Before the 1970 season, the team moved to Milwaukee and became the Brewers. The new team name came from beer making, a big deal in Milwaukee. The Brewers started out in the AL East Division. They moved to the AL Central from 1994 to 1997. In 1998, the team jumped to the NL Central!

Joe Schultz was the manager of the Pilots only season in 1969. ➤

WHO THEY PLAY

The Brewers play in the NL Central Division. The other teams in the NL Central are the Chicago Cubs, the Cincinnati Reds, the Pittsburgh Pirates, and the St. Louis Cardinals. The Brewers play more games against their division **rivals** than against other teams. In all, the Brewers play 162 games each season. They play 81 games at home and 81 on the road.

◄ *Jesús Aguilar was named to the NL All-Star team in 2018.*

WHERE THEY PLAY

The Brewers play in Miller Park. The team's home city can have hot summer weather. To keep fans cool, the ballpark has a roof that can open and close! The special roof means no more **rainouts**, either. Miller Park opened in 2001 and has been very popular. The Brewers have topped 2 million fans every season since 2004.

The huge arches above Miller Park hold the ➤
parts of the roof that open and close.

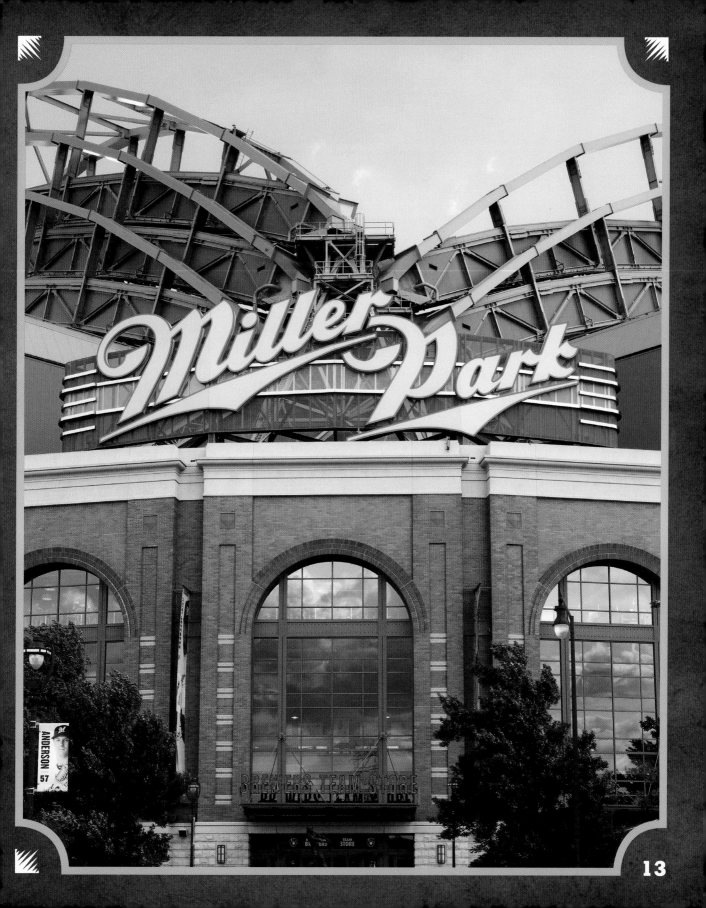

THE BASEBALL FIELD

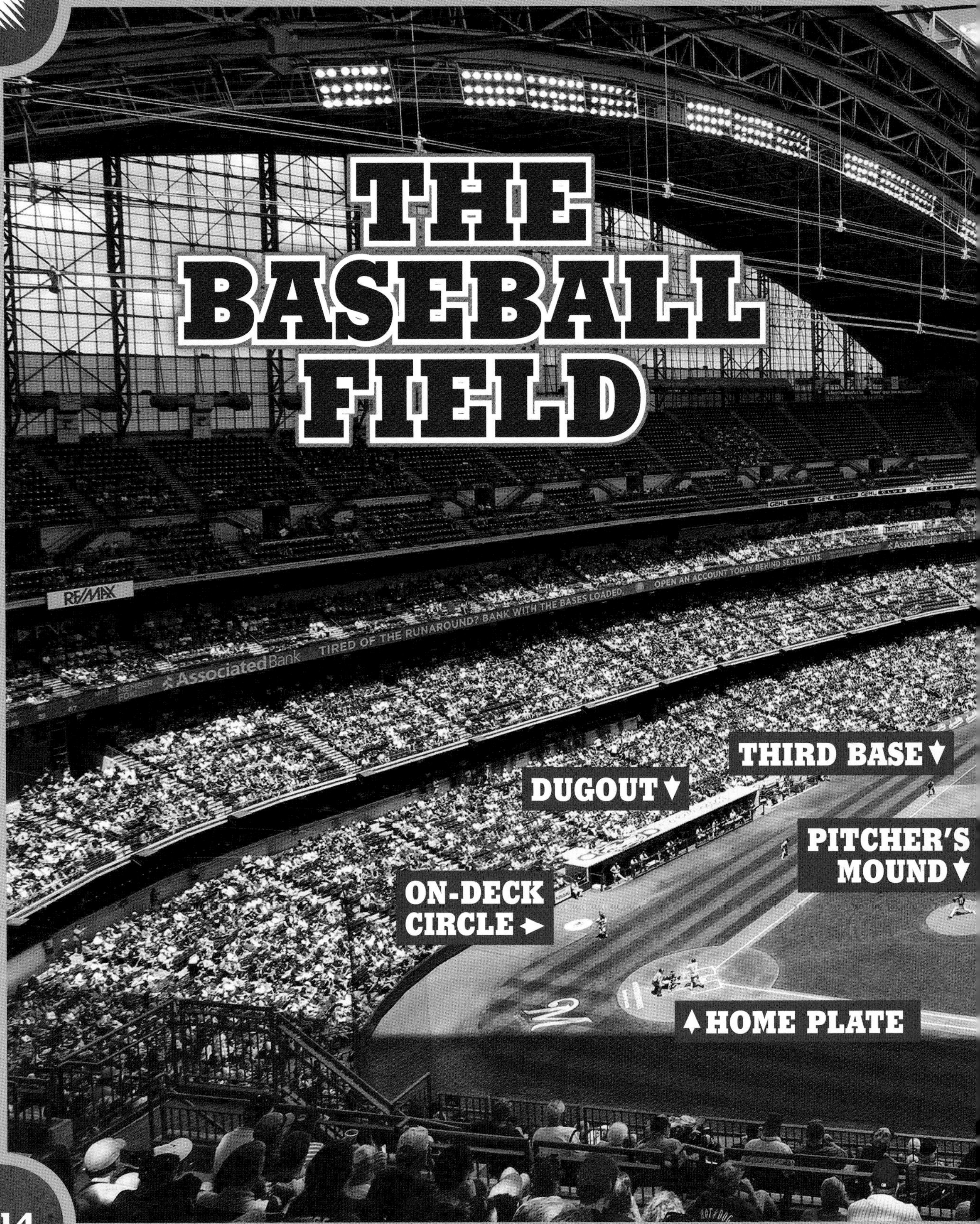

THIRD BASE ▼

DUGOUT ▼

PITCHER'S MOUND ▼

ON-DECK CIRCLE ▶

▲ HOME PLATE

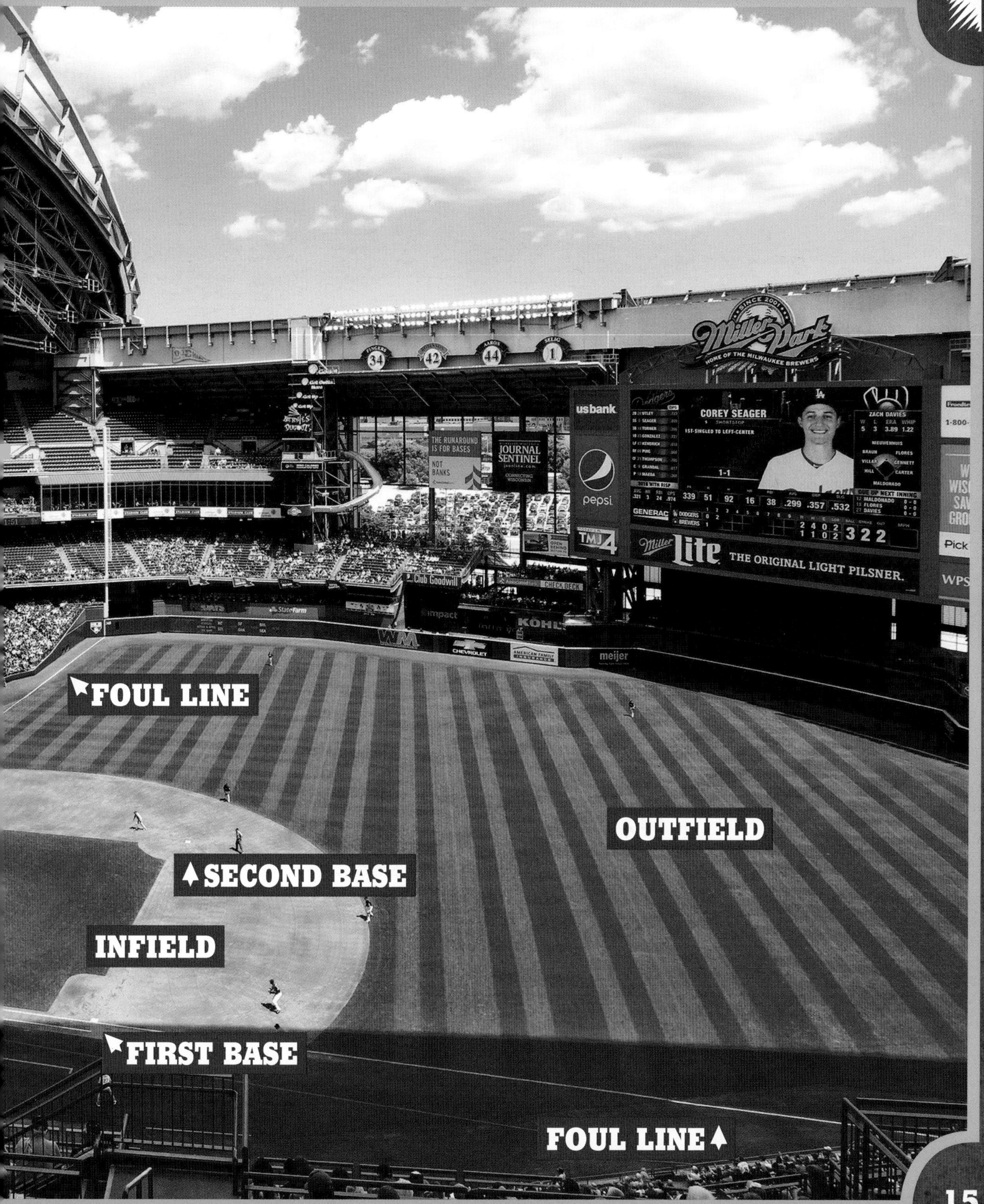

FOUL LINE
OUTFIELD
SECOND BASE
INFIELD
FIRST BASE
FOUL LINE
Miller Park
HOME OF THE MILWAUKEE BREWERS
SINCE 2001
COREY SEAGER
ZACH DAVIES
JOURNAL SENTINEL
THE RUNAROUND IS FOR BASES
NOT BANKS
usbank
pepsi
Miller Lite
THE ORIGINAL LIGHT PILSNER.

BIG DAYS

The Brewers have had a lot of great days in their long history. Here are a few of them.

1982—The Brewers won their only **pennant** this season. They won the AL East. Then they beat the California Angels in the playoffs. In the World Series, Milwaukee lost to the St. Louis Cardinals.

1975–1976—Hank Aaron was one of baseball's greatest sluggers. He played for the Atlanta Braves. That team began in Milwaukee before moving to Atlanta. In 1975, Aaron came back to Milwaukee to finish his career with the Brewers.

▲ *Milwaukee's Robin Yount lands after making a throw to first during the 1982 World Series.*

2011—Led by slugger Prince Fielder, Milwaukee won its first NL Central championship. In the playoffs, though, they lost to the Cardinals again!

TOUGH DAYS

L ike every team, the Brewers have had some not-so-great days, too. Here are a few their fans might not want to recall.

1998—Six pitchers couldn't do the job for Milwaukee. The Reds beat the Brewers 17–0, the team's worst loss ever!

2002—The Brewers have had some bad teams. This was the worst. The team lost 106 games, the most ever in one Brewers season.

2007—Brewers hitters had no answer for Justin Verlander. The Detroit Tigers **ace** threw a **no-hitter** against Milwaukee.

Geoff Jenkins is tagged out during one of ➤
Milwaukee's 106 losses in 2002.

MEET THE FANS!

Many people from Germany live near Milwaukee. They love to make and eat sausages. In 2000, Brewers fans began to enjoy a fun new game at the ballpark. Workers dressed in foam sausage costumes. Then they raced on the field between innings! Milwaukee's sausage races are popular with fans all over baseball.

◄ *Sausages from around the world take part in the Brewers races.*

HEROES THEN

Robin Yount was probably the best Brewers player ever. He won the Most Valuable Player Award as a shortstop and as an outfielder. Infielder Paul Molitor was a great hitter. He later became the manager of the Minnesota Twins. Prince Fielder smashed huge home runs! He hit 50 in 2007 to set a team record. Dan Plesac was a key pitcher in the late 1980s. He holds the team record for **saves**.

Paul Molitor was with Milwaukee from 1978 to ➤ *1992. He had 3,319 hits in his career.*

24

HEROES NOW

One of the Brewers' all-time greats is still on the team in 2018. Outfielder Ryan Braun smashes homers and steals bases. He holds several Brewers hitting records. Third baseman Travis Shaw is another Milwaukee slugger. Lorenzo Cain joined the team in 2017. He's a great base-stealer. Pitcher Josh Hader throws pitches faster than 100 miles per hour!

◀ *A broken bat didn't keep Travis Shaw from getting a hit in this 2018 game.*

GEARING UP

Baseball players wear team uniforms. On defense, they wear leather gloves to catch the ball. As batters, they wear hard helmets. This protects them from pitches. Batters hit the ball with long wood bats. Each player chooses his own size of bat. Catchers have the toughest job. They wear a lot of protection.

THE BASEBALL

The outside of the Major League baseball is made from cow leather. Two leather pieces shaped like 8s are stitched together. There are 108 stitches of red thread. These stitches help players grip the ball. Inside, the ball has a small center of cork and rubber. Hundreds of feet of yarn are tightly wound around this center.

◄ **CATCHER'S MASK AND HELMET**

CHEST PROTECTOR ►

◄ **PITCH CHART**

◄ **WRIST BANDS**

SHIN GUARDS ▲

◄ **CATCHER'S MITT**

CATCHER'S GEAR

TEAM STATS

Here are some of the all-time career records for the Milwaukee Brewers. All of these stats are through the 2018 regular season.

HOME RUNS

Ryan Braun	322
Robin Yount	251

STOLEN BASES

Paul Molitor	412
Robin Yount	271

BATTING AVERAGE

Jeff Cirillo	.307
Paul Molitor	.303

STRIKEOUTS

Yovani Gallardo	1,226
Ben Sheets	1,206

WINS

Jim Slaton	117
Mike Caldwell	102

SAVES

Dan Plesac	133
John Axford	106

Robin Yount spent his whole 20-year career with the Brewers. ➤

RBI

Robin Yount	1,406
Ryan Braun	1,053

GLOSSARY

ace (AYS) a team's top pitcher

no-hitter (no-HIT-er) a game in which the starting pitcher does not allow a hit to the opponent

pennant (PEN-nunt) a thin, pointed flag; it represents the winning team in the AL or NL each year

rainouts (RAYN-owts) games that are cancelled because of rain or storms

rivals (RYE-vulz) two people or groups competing for the same thing

World Series (WURLD SEE-reez) the annual championship of Major League Baseball

FIND OUT MORE

IN THE LIBRARY

Connery-Boyd, Peg. *Milwaukee Brewers: The Big Book of Activities*. Chicago, IL: Sourcebooks Jabberwocky, 2016.

Sports Illustrated for Kids (Editors). *Big Book of Who: Baseball*. New York, NY: Liberty Street, 2017.

Tavares, Matt. *Hank Aaron's Dream*.
Boston, MA: Candlewick, 2015.

ON THE WEB

Visit our website for links about the Milwaukee Brewers:
childsworld.com/links

Note to Parents, Teachers, and Librarians: We routinely verify our web links to make sure they are safe and active sites. So encourage your readers to check them out!

INDEX